371 Barker

Flower Fairies of the WINTER

Flower Fairies of the WINTER

Poems and pictures by

CICELY MARY BARKER

FREDERICK WARNE

FREDERICK WARNE

Published by the Penguin Group
Penguin Books Ltd, 80 Strand, London WC2R 0RL, England
Penguin Group (USA) Inc., 375 Hudson Street, New York, N.Y. 10014, USA
Penguin Books (Australia), 707 Collins Street,
Melbourne, Victoria 3008, Australia
Penguin Group (Canada), 90 Eglinton Avenue East,
Suite 700, Toronto, Ontario, Canada M4P 2Y3
Penguin Group (NZ), 67 Apollo Drive, Rosedale, North Shore 0632, New Zealand
Penguin Books India (Pty) Ltd, 11 Community Centre,
Panchsheel Park, New Delhi 110 017, India
Penguin Books (South Africa) (Pty) Ltd, Block D, Rosebank Office Park,
181 Jan Smuts Avenue, Parktown North, Gauteng, South Africa 2193

Penguin Books Ltd, Registered Offices: 80 Strand, London WC2R 0RL, England

www.flowerfairies.com

First published 1985
First published by Frederick Warne 1990
This edition published 2013

001

ISBN 978-0-14134-905-3

Printed in China

CONTENTS

The Snowdrop Fairy

THE SONG OF
THE SNOWDROP FAIRY

Deep sleeps the Winter,
    Cold, wet, and grey;
Surely all the world is dead;
    Spring is far away.
Wait! the world shall waken;
    It is not dead, for lo,
The Fair Maids of February
    Stand in the snow!

THE SONG OF
THE YEW FAIRY

Here, on the dark and solemn Yew,
　　A marvel may be seen,
Where waxen berries, pink and new,
　　Appear amid the green.

I sit a-dreaming in the tree,
　　So old and yet so new;
One hundred years, or two, or three
　　Are little to the Yew.

I think of bygone centuries,
　　And seem to see anew
The archers face their enemies
　　With bended bows of Yew.

The Yew Fairy

The Winter Jasmine Fairy

THE SONG OF
THE WINTER JASMINE FAIRY

All through the Summer my leaves were green,
But never a flower of mine was seen;
Now Summer is gone, that was so gay,
And my little green leaves are shed away.
     In the grey of the year
      What cheer, what cheer?

The Winter is come, the cold winds blow;
I shall feel the frost and the drifting snow;
But the sun can shine in December too,
And this is the time of my gift to you.
     See here, see here,
      My flowers appear!

The swallows have flown beyond the sea,
But friendly Robin, he stays with me;
And little Tom-Tit, so busy and small,
Hops where the jasmine is thick on the wall;
     And we say: "Good cheer!
      We're here! We're here!"

THE SONG OF
THE DEAD-NETTLE FAIRY

Through sun and rain, the country lane,
The field, the road, are my abode.
Though leaf and bud be splashed with mud,
Who cares? Not I!—I see the sky,
The kindly sun, the wayside fun
Of tramping folk who smoke and joke,
The bairns who heed my dusty weed
(No sting have I to make them cry),
And truth to tell, they love me well.
My brothers, White, and Yellow bright,
Are finer chaps than I, perhaps;
Who cares? Not I! So now good-bye.

The Dead-Nettle Fairy

The Rush-Grass and Cotton-Grass Fairies

THE SONG OF
THE RUSH-GRASS AND
COTTON-GRASS FAIRIES

Safe across the moorland
    Travellers may go,
If they heed our warning—
    We're the ones who know!

Let the footpath guide you—
    You'll be safely led;
There is bog beside you
    Where you cannot tread!

Mind where you are going!
    If you turn aside
Where you see us growing,
    Trouble will betide.

Keep you to the path, then!
    Hark to what we say!
Else, into the quagmire
    You will surely stray.

THE SONG OF
THE SPINDLE BERRY FAIRY

See the rosy-berried Spindle
All to sunset colours turning,
Till the thicket seems to kindle,
Just as though the trees were burning.
While my berries split and show
Orange-coloured seeds aglow,
One by one my leaves must fall:
Soon the wind will take them all.
Soon must fairies shut their eyes
For the Winter's hushabies;
But, before the Autumn goes,
Spindle turns to flame and rose!

The Spindle Berry Fairy

The Shepherd's-Purse Fairy

THE SONG OF
THE SHEPHERD'S-PURSE FAIRY

Though I'm poor to human eyes
Really I am rich and wise.
Every tiny flower I shed
Leaves a heart-shaped purse instead.

In each purse is wealth indeed—
Every coin a living seed.
Sow the seed upon the earth—
Living plants shall spring to birth.

Silly people's purses hold
Lifeless silver, clinking gold;
But you cannot grow a pound
From a farthing in the ground.

Money may become a curse:
Give me then my Shepherd's Purse.

THE SONG OF
THE GROUNDSEL FAIRY

If dicky-birds should buy and sell
In tiny markets, I can tell
    The way they'd spend their money.
They'd ask the price of cherries sweet,
They'd choose the pinkest worms for meat,
And common Groundsel for a treat,
    Though *you* might think it funny.

Love me not, or love me well;
That's the way they'd buy and sell.

The Groundsel Fairy

The Lords-and-Ladies Fairy

THE SONG OF
THE LORDS-AND-LADIES FAIRY

Fairies, when you lose your way,
    From the dance returning,
In the darkest undergrowth
    See my candles burning!
These shall make the pathway plain
    Homeward to your beds again.

(These are the berries of the Wild Arum, which has many
other names, and has a flower like a hood in the Spring.
The berries are not to be eaten.)

THE SONG OF
THE PLANE TREE FAIRY

You will not find him in the wood,
    Nor in the country lane;
But in the city's parks and streets
    You'll see the Plane.

O turn your eyes from pavements grey,
    And look you up instead,
To where the Plane tree's pretty balls
    Hang overhead!

When he has shed his golden leaves,
    His balls will yet remain,
To deck the tree until the Spring
    Comes back again!

The Plane Tree Fairy

The Burdock Fairy

THE SONG OF
THE BURDOCK FAIRY

Wee little hooks on each brown little bur,
(Mind where you're going, O Madam and Sir!)
How they will cling to your skirt-hem and stocking!
Hear how the Burdock is laughing and mocking:
Try to get rid of me, try as you will,
Shake me and scold me, I'll stick to you still,
      I'll stick to you still!

THE SONG OF
THE PINE TREE FAIRY

A tall, tall tree is the Pine tree,
　　With its trunk of bright red-brown—
The red of the merry squirrels
　　Who go scampering up and down.

There are cones on the tall, tall Pine tree,
　　With its needles sharp and green;
Small seeds in the cones are hidden,
　　And they ripen there unseen.

The elves play games with the squirrels
　　At the top of the tall, tall tree,
Throwing cones for the squirrels to nibble—
　　I wish I were there to see!

The Pine Tree Fairy

The Holly Fairy

THE SONG OF
THE HOLLY FAIRY

O, I am green in Winter-time,
    When other trees are brown;
Of all the trees (So saith the rhyme)
    The holly bears the crown.
December days are drawing near
    When I shall come to town,
And carol-boys go singing clear
Of all the trees (O hush and hear!)
    The holly bears the crown!

For who so well-beloved and merry
As the scarlet Holly Berry?

THE SONG OF
THE BOX TREE FAIRY

Have you seen the Box unclipped,
Never shaped and never snipped?
Often it's a garden hedge,
Just a narrow little edge;
Or in funny shapes it's cut,
And it's very pretty; *but*—

But, unclipped, it is a tree,
Growing as it likes to be;
And it has its blossoms too;
Tiny buds, the Winter through,
Wait to open in the Spring
In a scented yellow ring.

And among its leaves there play
Little blue-tits, brisk and gay.

The Box Tree Fairy

The Old-Man's-Beard Fairy

THE SONG OF
THE OLD-MAN'S-BEARD FAIRY

This is where the little elves
Cuddle down to hide themselves;
Into fluffy beds they creep,
Say good-night, and go to sleep.

(Old-Man's Beard is Wild Clematis; its flowers are called
Traveller's Joy. This silky fluff belongs to the seeds.)

THE SONG OF
THE BLACKTHORN FAIRY

The wind is cold, the Spring seems long
   a-waking;
  The woods are brown and bare;
Yet this is March: soon April will be making
  All things most sweet and fair.

See, even now, in hedge and thicket tangled,
  One brave and cheering sight:
The leafless branches of the Blackthorn,
   spangled
  With starry blossoms white!

(The cold days of March are sometimes called "Blackthorn Winter".)

The Blackthorn Fairy

The Hazel-Catkin Fairy

THE SONG OF
THE HAZEL-CATKIN FAIRY

Like little tails of little lambs,
    On leafless twigs my catkins swing;
They dingle-dangle merrily
    Before the wakening of Spring.

Beside the pollen-laden tails
    My tiny crimson tufts you see
The promise of the autumn nuts
    Upon the slender hazel tree.

While yet the woods lie grey and still
    I give my tidings: "Spring is near!"
One day the land shall leap to life
    With fairies calling: "Spring is HERE!"

THE SONG OF
THE TOTTER-GRASS FAIRY

The leaves on the tree-tops
  Dance in the breeze;
Totter-grass dances
  And sways like the trees—

Shaking and quaking!
  While through it there goes,
Dancing, a Fairy,
  On lightest of toes.

(Totter-grass is also called Quaking-grass.)

The Totter-Grass Fairy

The Winter Aconite Fairy

THE SONG OF
THE WINTER ACONITE FAIRY

Deep in the earth
I woke, I stirred.
I said: "Was that the Spring I heard?
For something called!"
"No, no," they said;
"Go back to sleep. Go back to bed.

"You're far too soon;
The world's too cold
For you, so small." So I was told.
But how could I
Go back to sleep?
I could not wait; I had to peep!

Up, up, I climbed,
And here am I.
How wide the earth! How great the sky!
O wintry world,
See me, awake!
Spring calls, and comes; 'tis no mistake.

THE SONG OF
THE CHRISTMAS TREE FAIRY

The little Christmas Tree was born
    And dwelt in open air;
It did not guess how bright a dress
    Some day its boughs would wear;
Brown cones were all, it thought, a tall
    And grown-up Fir would bear.

O little Fir! Your forest home
    Is far and far away;
And here indoors these boughs of yours
    With coloured balls are gay,
With candle-light, and tinsel bright,
    For this is Christmas Day!

A dolly-fairy stands on top,
    Till children sleep; then she
(A live one now!) from bough to bough
    Goes gliding silently.
O magic sight, this joyous night!
    O laden, sparkling tree!

The Christmas Tree Fairy

EDITOR'S NOTE

Cicely Mary Barker never compiled a
book of winter flower fairies herself,
although she painted many trees and
flowers which blossom during the
winter months. It was not until 1985,
12 years after her death, that *Flower
Fairies of the Winter* was compiled from
illustrations and poems in her other
7 Flower Fairies books. This edition
completes the quartet, so that there is
a Flower Fairies book for each season
of the year.